My Success Planner

Take Action Every Day To Win

Think
Plan
Change
Grow

By

Milca Exantus

Copyright © 2019 Milca Exantus

All rights reserved. Except as permitted by copyright laws, no part of this book may be reprinted or reproduced in any form or by any electronic, mechanical, or other means, now known or hereafter invented, including photocopying, recording and information storage and retrieved, without permission from the publisher.

ISBN: 9781670930149

My Success Planner
Take Action Every Day to Win

Acknowledgement
Letter to Readers

Section 1: Defining Success 1

Section 2: Know your Dreams, Desires and Goals...3

Section 3: Self-Discovery for Success……………..7

Section. 4: Monthly, Weekly, Daily Goals…………11

Sections 5: Reflections and Wins………………….151

Acknowledgements

I offer my sincere gratitude to my mom and dad who helped me discover the love and joy of learning. Thank you to all my family, friends, colleagues, students, and Book Coach Chanell Fair you who helped inspired this book.

With Love,

Milca Exantus

Dear Readers,

Thank you for believing in your success. Your Success is needed to make an impact in the world. I hope you will enjoy using this planner daily to achieve your goals and see your dreams come to life.

Planning is important to achieve success. This planner targets, positive thinking, emotional success and goal setting. Start each day with a positive thought, scripture, or affirmation to practice throughout the day. Next, understand your feelings, attitude, and mood. Be prepared with positive strategies to overcome negative emotions. Do not allow negative emotions to overwhelm you.

Make your goals and expectations clear for your relationships. Be ready to compromise and negotiate to build healthy relationships. Focus on improving your connections, communication, and intimacy in your relationships.

Celebrate your wins every day. Be proud of what you accomplish and continue to improve and grow. Do not be discouraged when you don't achieve all your targets. Create new opportunities to move forward. Celebrate your successes with love ones. Continue to make the changes that will bring success. Wishing you much success!

With Love,
Milca Exantus

Section 1

Defining Success

Success is a process that can bring joy and happiness.
Success is working hard to see the results and outcomes you desire.
Success is feeling satisfaction and contentment.

Success is being focused not busy.
Success is overcoming challenges and obstacles.
Success is always changing and growing.
Success is forgiving the past and focused on the present.
Success is being excited about the future.

Success is being disciplined, committed, confident, and bold.
Success is challenging yourself to go above and beyond the expectations.
Success is not being afraid of what others think or say about your dreams.
Success is knowing when to go strong and when to relax.
Success is changing the brain to create new ideas and innovations.
Success is being excited about learning and maturing.

Success is knowing who you are and who you want to become.
Success is knowing when to recharge and destress.
Success is sharing your gifts, talents, and skills.
Success is being receptive to suggestions.

Success is eagerness to learn something new every day.
Success is learning from past mistakes and failures.
Success is taking risks.
Success is moving forward after disappointments.
Success is taking action to achieve goals.

Success is believing in others and working well with others.
Success is being a leader.
Success is being compassionate and helping others.
Success is loving and serving others. Success is understanding others.

Success is finding balance in life.
Success is understanding your emotions and the emotions of others.
Success is having a positive mindset.
Success is health, fitness and wellness.
Success is loving and caring for others.
Success is believing all things are possible.
Success is Powerful. Be Successful!

What is your Definition of Success? Why?

Section 2

Know your Dreams, Desires and Goals

Being specific and clear on what your dreams and goals are is important to achieving success. Our dreams and goals motivate us to take action to see results in our lives. It is critical to take time to clearly define what you would like to see in your life and why. When you can answer why you want to pursue your dreams, you are likely to achieve your goals.

This section is designed to give you the space to think about your dreams and goals and what they mean to you. Don't be afraid to write down your big dreams, goals and desires. Even if they seem impossible, write them down. Sometimes when our dreams are written down it builds confidence to move towards success.

The first step is knowing exactly what you want to achieve and why this is meaningful to you. Once you are specific and clear, then it is time to take action to see the results. Do not be discouraged if your dreams, goals, vision, or ideas are not understood. Your dreams should excite you every day. Do not allow fear or doubt stop you from creating an amazing life. We are designed to experience a successful life. When you think about your life and where you are going, create and exciting vision. Continue to plan even if you do not know how it will happen.

Use your imagination to dream about places you want to go and things you want to achieve even if you currently do not have the skills. Think about how can learn new skills necessary to achieve your goals. Your dreams and desires should motivate you to keep learning and growing. You might not have the skills now to achieve your dreams and goals, but you can develop new skills,

Go ahead and write down those big goals and dreams. Don't hold back. Believe that you are able of achieve your dreams. Write them down daily and monitor your progress. Make necessary changes to see your success.

Let's get going!!!

Goals: What I want to achieve? What are my dreams and desires?	Why?

Goals: What I want to achieve? What are my dreams and desires?	Why?

Goals: What I want to achieve? What are my dreams and desires?	Why?

Section 3

Self-Discovery for Success

Success is a process of discovering your strengths and weakness. Self-discovery allows you to continue to grow and learn. We should constantly learn something new about who we are and who we are becoming. It is necessary to get out of our comfort zone.

There are always new things that we can learn and there are always areas in our lives that we can change. Self-discovery challenges us to take risks and become receptive to change. We are not created to remain the same. We will grow and seasons will change. Are you comfortable with change?

Life is designed with challenges and obstacles. As we take on new challenges and obstacles, we develop new skills and knowledge. Do not get too comfortable with what you know. Develop a passion to learn and discover new information.

We should be excited about the new opportunities. Working with others also help us develop new skills and understanding. We can learn how to communicate and solve problems when we work with others.

Fear and doubt can keep us from pursuing our goals and dreams. Remember it is ok to keep changing, growing, and improving. Do not get too comfortable with who you are. We can improve at every stage in life. Always seek opportunities to take your life to the next level. This will drive you forward to achieving success. Being successful is enjoyable even when you must work to get it. Discovering your strengths should move you towards new adventures every day.

Self-Discovery for Success

How would you describe who you are now?

How would you describe who you want to become?

Self-Discovery for Success

Strengths	Weakness	New Skills to Develop

FEARS	CHALLENGES	OBSTALCES

Section 4

Planning for Success

Planning is process of developing action steps to achieve your goals and dreams. It is important to write down your plans every day. Without a plan it is difficult to measure success. Success is driven by clear and concise plans. Success is about seeing results and outcomes. It is critical to write down clear plans for each month, week, and day.

Life can become overwhelming without clear plans on what actions are needed to achieve our goals. There are many areas of life such as family, work, relationships, health and fitness. It is important to find balance and achieve success in all areas of life.

In this section, you can set big goals and set action steps daily to achieve those goals. It is important to start each day with clear expectations. Without clear expectations and targets, a lot of time can be wasted. Check in with your goals frequently throughout the day. When you see the achievements daily, that will give you confidence and motivation to continue to move forward.

It is also important to be flexible. Things can change throughout the day. Keep an open mind set on how to approach challenges and obstacles that may arise throughout the day. Being positive about your progress to achieve your goals is important. Celebrate small wins every day. Do not get discouraged if you must make changes to your plans. Start with your monthly goals and develop a habit to set weekly and daily goals to see results.

Monthly Goals	**Month:**	**Year:**

Monthly Goals	**Month:**	**Year:**

Monthly Goals	**Month:**	**Year:**

Monthly Goals	**Month:**	**Year:**

Monthly Goals	Month:	Year:

Monthly Goals	Month:	Year:

Monthly Goals	Month:	Year:

Monthly Goals	Month:	Year:

Monthly Goals	**Month:**	**Year:**

Monthly Goals	**Month:**	**Year:**

Monthly Goals	**Month:**	**Year:**

Monthly Goals	**Month:**	**Year:**

Month: **Week:**

Month: **Week:**

Month: **Week:**

Month: **Week:**

Month: **Week:**

Month: **Week:**

Month: **Week:**

Month: **Week:**

Month: **Week:**

Month: **Week:**

Month: **Week:**

Month: **Week:**

Month: **Week:**

Month: **Week:**

Month: **Week:**

Month: **Week:**

Month: **Week:**

Month: **Week:**

Month: **Week:**

Month: **Week:**

Month: **Week:**

Month: **Week:**

Month: **Week:**

Month: **Week:**

Month: **Week:**

Month: **Week:**

Month: **Week:**

Month: **Week:**

Month: **Week:**

Month: **Week:**

Month: **Week:**

Month: **Week:**

Date: _____

My Success Planner
Take Action Every Day to Win

Mindset Goals: What positive thoughts will I have today?

Emotional Goals: What positive actions will I take today to feel joy and happiness?

Health/ Fitness/ Wellness Goals: What can I do today to improve my health, wellness, and fitness?

Relationship Goals: What can I do today to improve my relationships?

Personal/ Professional Goals: What can I do today to reach my school, professional, business, or financial goals?

Celebrate Wins: What are you most proud of today?

Improvements: What changes are necessary now?

Date: _____

**My Success Planner
Take Action Every Day to Win**

Mindset Goals: What positive thoughts will I have today?

Emotional Goals: What positive actions will I take today to feel joy and happiness?

Health/ Fitness/ Wellness Goals: What can I do today to improve my health, wellness, and fitness?

Relationship Goals: What can I do today to improve my relationships?

Personal/ Professional Goals: What can I do today to reach my school, professional, business, or financial goals?

Celebrate Wins: What are you most proud of today?

Improvements: What changes are necessary now?

Date: _____

**My Success Planner
Take Action Every Day to Win**

Mindset Goals: What positive thoughts will I have today?

Emotional Goals: What positive actions will I take today to feel joy and happiness?

Health/ Fitness/ Wellness Goals: What can I do today to improve my health, wellness, and fitness?

Relationship Goals: What can I do today to improve my relationships?

Personal/ Professional Goals: What can I do today to reach my school, professional, business, or financial goals?

Celebrate Wins: What are you most proud of today?

Improvements: What changes are necessary now?

Date: _____

> **My Success Planner**
> **Take Action Every Day to Win**

Mindset Goals: What positive thoughts will I have today?

Emotional Goals: What positive actions will I take today to feel joy and happiness?

Health/ Fitness/ Wellness Goals: What can I do today to improve my health, wellness, and fitness?

Relationship Goals: What can I do today to improve my relationships?

Personal/ Professional Goals: What can I do today to reach my school, professional, business, or financial goals?

Celebrate Wins: What are you most proud of today?

Improvements: What changes are necessary now?

Date: _____

| **My Success Planner** |
| **Take Action Every Day to Win** |

Mindset Goals: What positive thoughts will I have today?
___
___
___

Emotional Goals: What positive actions will I take today to feel joy and happiness?
___
___
___

Health/ Fitness/ Wellness Goals: What can I do today to improve my health, wellness, and fitness?
___
___
___

Relationship Goals: What can I do today to improve my relationships?
___
___
___

Personal/ Professional Goals: What can I do today to reach my school, professional, business, or financial goals?
___
___
___

Celebrate Wins: What are you most proud of today?
___

Improvements: What changes are necessary now?
___

Date: _____

My Success Planner
Take Action Every Day to Win

Mindset Goals: What positive thoughts will I have today?

Emotional Goals: What positive actions will I take today to feel joy and happiness?

Health/ Fitness/ Wellness Goals: What can I do today to improve my health, wellness, and fitness?

Relationship Goals: What can I do today to improve my relationships?

Personal/ Professional Goals: What can I do today to reach my school, professional, business, or financial goals?

Celebrate Wins: What are you most proud of today?

Improvements: What changes are necessary now?

Date: _____

**My Success Planner
Take Action Every Day to Win**

Mindset Goals: What positive thoughts will I have today?

Emotional Goals: What positive actions will I take today to feel joy and happiness?

Health/ Fitness/ Wellness Goals: What can I do today to improve my health, wellness, and fitness?

Relationship Goals: What can I do today to improve my relationships?

Personal/ Professional Goals: What can I do today to reach my school, professional, business, or financial goals?

Celebrate Wins: What are you most proud of today?

Improvements: What changes are necessary now?

Date: _____

> **My Success Planner**
> **Take Action Every Day to Win**

Mindset Goals: What positive thoughts will I have today?

Emotional Goals: What positive actions will I take today to feel joy and happiness?

Health/ Fitness/ Wellness Goals: What can I do today to improve my health, wellness, and fitness?

Relationship Goals: What can I do today to improve my relationships?

Personal/ Professional Goals: What can I do today to reach my school, professional, business, or financial goals?

Celebrate Wins: What are you most proud of today?

Improvements: What changes are necessary now?

Date: _____

My Success Planner
Take Action Every Day to Win

Mindset Goals: What positive thoughts will I have today?

Emotional Goals: What positive actions will I take today to feel joy and happiness?

Health/ Fitness/ Wellness Goals: What can I do today to improve my health, wellness, and fitness?

Relationship Goals: What can I do today to improve my relationships?

Personal/ Professional Goals: What can I do today to reach my school, professional, business, or financial goals?

Celebrate Wins: What are you most proud of today?

Improvements: What changes are necessary now?

Date: _____

My Success Planner
Take Action Every Day to Win

Mindset Goals: What positive thoughts will I have today?

_____
_____
_____

Emotional Goals: What positive actions will I take today to feel joy and happiness?

_____
_____
_____

Health/ Fitness/ Wellness Goals: What can I do today to improve my health, wellness, and fitness?

_____
_____
_____

Relationship Goals: What can I do today to improve my relationships?

_____
_____
_____

Personal/ Professional Goals: What can I do today to reach my school, professional, business, or financial goals?

_____
_____
_____

Celebrate Wins: What are you most proud of today?

_____

Improvements: What changes are necessary now?

_____

Date: _____

**My Success Planner
Take Action Every Day to Win**

Mindset Goals: What positive thoughts will I have today?

Emotional Goals: What positive actions will I take today to feel joy and happiness?

Health/ Fitness/ Wellness Goals: What can I do today to improve my health, wellness, and fitness?

Relationship Goals: What can I do today to improve my relationships?

Personal/ Professional Goals: What can I do today to reach my school, professional, business, or financial goals?

Celebrate Wins: What are you most proud of today?

Improvements: What changes are necessary now?

Date: _____

My Success Planner
Take Action Every Day to Win

Mindset Goals: What positive thoughts will I have today?

Emotional Goals: What positive actions will I take today to feel joy and happiness?

Health/ Fitness/ Wellness Goals: What can I do today to improve my health, wellness, and fitness?

Relationship Goals: What can I do today to improve my relationships?

Personal/ Professional Goals: What can I do today to reach my school, professional, business, or financial goals?

Celebrate Wins: What are you most proud of today?

Improvements: What changes are necessary now?

Date: _____

**My Success Planner
Take Action Every Day to Win**

Mindset Goals: What positive thoughts will I have today?

Emotional Goals: What positive actions will I take today to feel joy and happiness?

Health/ Fitness/ Wellness Goals: What can I do today to improve my health, wellness, and fitness?

Relationship Goals: What can I do today to improve my relationships?

Personal/ Professional Goals: What can I do today to reach my school, professional, business, or financial goals?

Celebrate Wins: What are you most proud of today?

Improvements: What changes are necessary now?

Date: _____

My Success Planner
Take Action Every Day to Win

Mindset Goals: What positive thoughts will I have today?

Emotional Goals: What positive actions will I take today to feel joy and happiness?

Health/ Fitness/ Wellness Goals: What can I do today to improve my health, wellness, and fitness?

Relationship Goals: What can I do today to improve my relationships?

Personal/ Professional Goals: What can I do today to reach my school, professional, business, or financial goals?

Celebrate Wins: What are you most proud of today?

Improvements: What changes are necessary now?

Date: _____

My Success Planner
Take Action Every Day to Win

Mindset Goals: What positive thoughts will I have today?
_____
_____
_____

Emotional Goals: What positive actions will I take today to feel joy and happiness?
_____
_____
_____

Health/ Fitness/ Wellness Goals: What can I do today to improve my health, wellness, and fitness?
_____
_____
_____

Relationship Goals: What can I do today to improve my relationships?
_____
_____
_____

Personal/ Professional Goals: What can I do today to reach my school, professional, business, or financial goals?
_____
_____
_____

Celebrate Wins: What are you most proud of today?
_____

Improvements: What changes are necessary now?
_____

Date: _____

My Success Planner
Take Action Every Day to Win

Mindset Goals: What positive thoughts will I have today?

Emotional Goals: What positive actions will I take today to feel joy and happiness?

Health/ Fitness/ Wellness Goals: What can I do today to improve my health, wellness, and fitness?

Relationship Goals: What can I do today to improve my relationships?

Personal/ Professional Goals: What can I do today to reach my school, professional, business, or financial goals?

Celebrate Wins: What are you most proud of today?

Improvements: What changes are necessary now?

Date: _____

**My Success Planner
Take Action Every Day to Win**

Mindset Goals: What positive thoughts will I have today?

Emotional Goals: What positive actions will I take today to feel joy and happiness?

Health/ Fitness/ Wellness Goals: What can I do today to improve my health, wellness, and fitness?

Relationship Goals: What can I do today to improve my relationships?

Personal/ Professional Goals: What can I do today to reach my school, professional, business, or financial goals?

Celebrate Wins: What are you most proud of today?

Improvements: What changes are necessary now?

Date: _____

**My Success Planner
Take Action Every Day to Win**

Mindset Goals: What positive thoughts will I have today?

Emotional Goals: What positive actions will I take today to feel joy and happiness?

Health/ Fitness/ Wellness Goals: What can I do today to improve my health, wellness, and fitness?

Relationship Goals: What can I do today to improve my relationships?

Personal/ Professional Goals: What can I do today to reach my school, professional, business, or financial goals?

Celebrate Wins: What are you most proud of today?

Improvements: What changes are necessary now?

Date: _____

**My Success Planner
Take Action Every Day to Win**

Mindset Goals: What positive thoughts will I have today?

Emotional Goals: What positive actions will I take today to feel joy and happiness?

Health/ Fitness/ Wellness Goals: What can I do today to improve my health, wellness, and fitness?

Relationship Goals: What can I do today to improve my relationships?

Personal/ Professional Goals: What can I do today to reach my school, professional, business, or financial goals?

Celebrate Wins: What are you most proud of today?

Improvements: What changes are necessary now?

Date: _____

**My Success Planner
Take Action Every Day to Win**

Mindset Goals: What positive thoughts will I have today?

Emotional Goals: What positive actions will I take today to feel joy and happiness?

Health/ Fitness/ Wellness Goals: What can I do today to improve my health, wellness, and fitness?

Relationship Goals: What can I do today to improve my relationships?

Personal/ Professional Goals: What can I do today to reach my school, professional, business, or financial goals?

Celebrate Wins: What are you most proud of today?

Improvements: What changes are necessary now?

Date: _____

> **My Success Planner**
> **Take Action Every Day to Win**

Mindset Goals: What positive thoughts will I have today?

Emotional Goals: What positive actions will I take today to feel joy and happiness?

Health/ Fitness/ Wellness Goals: What can I do today to improve my health, wellness, and fitness?

Relationship Goals: What can I do today to improve my relationships?

Personal/ Professional Goals: What can I do today to reach my school, professional, business, or financial goals?

Celebrate Wins: What are you most proud of today?

Improvements: What changes are necessary now?

Date: _____

**My Success Planner
Take Action Every Day to Win**

Mindset Goals: What positive thoughts will I have today?

Emotional Goals: What positive actions will I take today to feel joy and happiness?

Health/ Fitness/ Wellness Goals: What can I do today to improve my health, wellness, and fitness?

Relationship Goals: What can I do today to improve my relationships?

Personal/ Professional Goals: What can I do today to reach my school, professional, business, or financial goals?

Celebrate Wins: What are you most proud of today?

Improvements: What changes are necessary now?

Date: _____

**My Success Planner
Take Action Every Day to Win**

Mindset Goals: What positive thoughts will I have today?

Emotional Goals: What positive actions will I take today to feel joy and happiness?

Health/ Fitness/ Wellness Goals: What can I do today to improve my health, wellness, and fitness?

Relationship Goals: What can I do today to improve my relationships?

Personal/ Professional Goals: What can I do today to reach my school, professional, business, or financial goals?

Celebrate Wins: What are you most proud of today?

Improvements: What changes are necessary now?

Date: _____

| My Success Planner |
| Take Action Every Day to Win |

Mindset Goals: What positive thoughts will I have today?

Emotional Goals: What positive actions will I take today to feel joy and happiness?

Health/ Fitness/ Wellness Goals: What can I do today to improve my health, wellness, and fitness?

Relationship Goals: What can I do today to improve my relationships?

Personal/ Professional Goals: What can I do today to reach my school, professional, business, or financial goals?

Celebrate Wins: What are you most proud of today?

Improvements: What changes are necessary now?

My Success Planner
Take Action Every Day to Win

Date: _____

Mindset Goals: What positive thoughts will I have today?

Emotional Goals: What positive actions will I take today to feel joy and happiness?

Health/ Fitness/ Wellness Goals: What can I do today to improve my health, wellness, and fitness?

Relationship Goals: What can I do today to improve my relationships?

Personal/ Professional Goals: What can I do today to reach my school, professional, business, or financial goals?

Celebrate Wins: What are you most proud of today?

Improvements: What changes are necessary now?

Date: _____

My Success Planner
Take Action Every Day to Win

Mindset Goals: What positive thoughts will I have today?

Emotional Goals: What positive actions will I take today to feel joy and happiness?

Health/ Fitness/ Wellness Goals: What can I do today to improve my health, wellness, and fitness?

Relationship Goals: What can I do today to improve my relationships?

Personal/ Professional Goals: What can I do today to reach my school, professional, business, or financial goals?

Celebrate Wins: What are you most proud of today?

Improvements: What changes are necessary now?

Date: _____

**My Success Planner
Take Action Every Day to Win**

Mindset Goals: What positive thoughts will I have today?

Emotional Goals: What positive actions will I take today to feel joy and happiness?

Health/ Fitness/ Wellness Goals: What can I do today to improve my health, wellness, and fitness?

Relationship Goals: What can I do today to improve my relationships?

Personal/ Professional Goals: What can I do today to reach my school, professional, business, or financial goals?

Celebrate Wins: What are you most proud of today?

Improvements: What changes are necessary now?

Date: _____

**My Success Planner
Take Action Every Day to Win**

Mindset Goals: What positive thoughts will I have today?

Emotional Goals: What positive actions will I take today to feel joy and happiness?

Health/ Fitness/ Wellness Goals: What can I do today to improve my health, wellness, and fitness?

Relationship Goals: What can I do today to improve my relationships?

Personal/ Professional Goals: What can I do today to reach my school, professional, business, or financial goals?

Celebrate Wins: What are you most proud of today?

Improvements: What changes are necessary now?

Date: _____

> **My Success Planner**
> **Take Action Every Day to Win**

Mindset Goals: What positive thoughts will I have today?

Emotional Goals: What positive actions will I take today to feel joy and happiness?

Health/ Fitness/ Wellness Goals: What can I do today to improve my health, wellness, and fitness?

Relationship Goals: What can I do today to improve my relationships?

Personal/ Professional Goals: What can I do today to reach my school, professional, business, or financial goals?

Celebrate Wins: What are you most proud of today?

Improvements: What changes are necessary now?

Date: _____

My Success Planner
Take Action Every Day to Win

Mindset Goals: What positive thoughts will I have today?

Emotional Goals: What positive actions will I take today to feel joy and happiness?

Health/ Fitness/ Wellness Goals: What can I do today to improve my health, wellness, and fitness?

Relationship Goals: What can I do today to improve my relationships?

Personal/ Professional Goals: What can I do today to reach my school, professional, business, or financial goals?

Celebrate Wins: What are you most proud of today?

Improvements: What changes are necessary now?

Date: _____

> **My Success Planner**
> **Take Action Every Day to Win**

Mindset Goals: What positive thoughts will I have today?

Emotional Goals: What positive actions will I take today to feel joy and happiness?

Health/ Fitness/ Wellness Goals: What can I do today to improve my health, wellness, and fitness?

Relationship Goals: What can I do today to improve my relationships?

Personal/ Professional Goals: What can I do today to reach my school, professional, business, or financial goals?

Celebrate Wins: What are you most proud of today?

Improvements: What changes are necessary now?

Date: _____

**My Success Planner
Take Action Every Day to Win**

Mindset Goals: What positive thoughts will I have today?

Emotional Goals: What positive actions will I take today to feel joy and happiness?

Health/ Fitness/ Wellness Goals: What can I do today to improve my health, wellness, and fitness?

Relationship Goals: What can I do today to improve my relationships?

Personal/ Professional Goals: What can I do today to reach my school, professional, business, or financial goals?

Celebrate Wins: What are you most proud of today?

Improvements: What changes are necessary now?

Date: _____

My Success Planner
Take Action Every Day to Win

Mindset Goals: What positive thoughts will I have today?

Emotional Goals: What positive actions will I take today to feel joy and happiness?

Health/ Fitness/ Wellness Goals: What can I do today to improve my health, wellness, and fitness?

Relationship Goals: What can I do today to improve my relationships?

Personal/ Professional Goals: What can I do today to reach my school, professional, business, or financial goals?

Celebrate Wins: What are you most proud of today?

Improvements: What changes are necessary now?

Date: _____

**My Success Planner
Take Action Every Day to Win**

Mindset Goals: What positive thoughts will I have today?

Emotional Goals: What positive actions will I take today to feel joy and happiness?

Health/ Fitness/ Wellness Goals: What can I do today to improve my health, wellness, and fitness?

Relationship Goals: What can I do today to improve my relationships?

Personal/ Professional Goals: What can I do today to reach my school, professional, business, or financial goals?

Celebrate Wins: What are you most proud of today?

Improvements: What changes are necessary now?

Date: _____

**My Success Planner
Take Action Every Day to Win**

Mindset Goals: What positive thoughts will I have today?

Emotional Goals: What positive actions will I take today to feel joy and happiness?

Health/ Fitness/ Wellness Goals: What can I do today to improve my health, wellness, and fitness?

Relationship Goals: What can I do today to improve my relationships?

Personal/ Professional Goals: What can I do today to reach my school, professional, business, or financial goals?

Celebrate Wins: What are you most proud of today?

Improvements: What changes are necessary now?

Date: _____

**My Success Planner
Take Action Every Day to Win**

Mindset Goals: What positive thoughts will I have today?

Emotional Goals: What positive actions will I take today to feel joy and happiness?

Health/ Fitness/ Wellness Goals: What can I do today to improve my health, wellness, and fitness?

Relationship Goals: What can I do today to improve my relationships?

Personal/ Professional Goals: What can I do today to reach my school, professional, business, or financial goals?

Celebrate Wins: What are you most proud of today?

Improvements: What changes are necessary now?

Date: _____

**My Success Planner
Take Action Every Day to Win**

Mindset Goals: What positive thoughts will I have today?

Emotional Goals: What positive actions will I take today to feel joy and happiness?

Health/ Fitness/ Wellness Goals: What can I do today to improve my health, wellness, and fitness?

Relationship Goals: What can I do today to improve my relationships?

Personal/ Professional Goals: What can I do today to reach my school, professional, business, or financial goals?

Celebrate Wins: What are you most proud of today?

Improvements: What changes are necessary now?

Date: _____

My Success Planner
Take Action Every Day to Win

Mindset Goals: What positive thoughts will I have today?

Emotional Goals: What positive actions will I take today to feel joy and happiness?

Health/ Fitness/ Wellness Goals: What can I do today to improve my health, wellness, and fitness?

Relationship Goals: What can I do today to improve my relationships?

Personal/ Professional Goals: What can I do today to reach my school, professional, business, or financial goals?

Celebrate Wins: What are you most proud of today?

Improvements: What changes are necessary now?

Date: _____

**My Success Planner
Take Action Every Day to Win**

Mindset Goals: What positive thoughts will I have today?

Emotional Goals: What positive actions will I take today to feel joy and happiness?

Health/ Fitness/ Wellness Goals: What can I do today to improve my health, wellness, and fitness?

Relationship Goals: What can I do today to improve my relationships?

Personal/ Professional Goals: What can I do today to reach my school, professional, business, or financial goals?

Celebrate Wins: What are you most proud of today?

Improvements: What changes are necessary now?

Date: _____

> **My Success Planner**
> **Take Action Every Day to Win**

Mindset Goals: What positive thoughts will I have today?

Emotional Goals: What positive actions will I take today to feel joy and happiness?

Health/ Fitness/ Wellness Goals: What can I do today to improve my health, wellness, and fitness?

Relationship Goals: What can I do today to improve my relationships?

Personal/ Professional Goals: What can I do today to reach my school, professional, business, or financial goals?

Celebrate Wins: What are you most proud of today?

Improvements: What changes are necessary now?

Date: _____

My Success Planner
Take Action Every Day to Win

Mindset Goals: What positive thoughts will I have today?

Emotional Goals: What positive actions will I take today to feel joy and happiness?

Health/ Fitness/ Wellness Goals: What can I do today to improve my health, wellness, and fitness?

Relationship Goals: What can I do today to improve my relationships?

Personal/ Professional Goals: What can I do today to reach my school, professional, business, or financial goals?

Celebrate Wins: What are you most proud of today?

Improvements: What changes are necessary now?

Date: _____

My Success Planner
Take Action Every Day to Win

Mindset Goals: What positive thoughts will I have today?

Emotional Goals: What positive actions will I take today to feel joy and happiness?

Health/ Fitness/ Wellness Goals: What can I do today to improve my health, wellness, and fitness?

Relationship Goals: What can I do today to improve my relationships?

Personal/ Professional Goals: What can I do today to reach my school, professional, business, or financial goals?

Celebrate Wins: What are you most proud of today?

Improvements: What changes are necessary now?

Date: _____

My Success Planner
Take Action Every Day to Win

Mindset Goals: What positive thoughts will I have today?

Emotional Goals: What positive actions will I take today to feel joy and happiness?

Health/ Fitness/ Wellness Goals: What can I do today to improve my health, wellness, and fitness?

Relationship Goals: What can I do today to improve my relationships?

Personal/ Professional Goals: What can I do today to reach my school, professional, business, or financial goals?

Celebrate Wins: What are you most proud of today?

Improvements: What changes are necessary now?

My Success Planner
Take Action Every Day to Win

Date: _____

Mindset Goals: What positive thoughts will I have today?

Emotional Goals: What positive actions will I take today to feel joy and happiness?

Health/ Fitness/ Wellness Goals: What can I do today to improve my health, wellness, and fitness?

Relationship Goals: What can I do today to improve my relationships?

Personal/ Professional Goals: What can I do today to reach my school, professional, business, or financial goals?

Celebrate Wins: What are you most proud of today?

Improvements: What changes are necessary now?

Date: _____

My Success Planner
Take Action Every Day to Win

Mindset Goals: What positive thoughts will I have today?

Emotional Goals: What positive actions will I take today to feel joy and happiness?

Health/ Fitness/ Wellness Goals: What can I do today to improve my health, wellness, and fitness?

Relationship Goals: What can I do today to improve my relationships?

Personal/ Professional Goals: What can I do today to reach my school, professional, business, or financial goals?

Celebrate Wins: What are you most proud of today?

Improvements: What changes are necessary now?

Date: _____

My Success Planner
Take Action Every Day to Win

Mindset Goals: What positive thoughts will I have today?

Emotional Goals: What positive actions will I take today to feel joy and happiness?

Health/ Fitness/ Wellness Goals: What can I do today to improve my health, wellness, and fitness?

Relationship Goals: What can I do today to improve my relationships?

Personal/ Professional Goals: What can I do today to reach my school, professional, business, or financial goals?

Celebrate Wins: What are you most proud of today?

Improvements: What changes are necessary now?

Date: _____

> **My Success Planner**
> **Take Action Every Day to Win**

Mindset Goals: What positive thoughts will I have today?

Emotional Goals: What positive actions will I take today to feel joy and happiness?

Health/ Fitness/ Wellness Goals: What can I do today to improve my health, wellness, and fitness?

Relationship Goals: What can I do today to improve my relationships?

Personal/ Professional Goals: What can I do today to reach my school, professional, business, or financial goals?

Celebrate Wins: What are you most proud of today?

Improvements: What changes are necessary now?

Date: _____

**My Success Planner
Take Action Every Day to Win**

Mindset Goals: What positive thoughts will I have today?

Emotional Goals: What positive actions will I take today to feel joy and happiness?

Health/ Fitness/ Wellness Goals: What can I do today to improve my health, wellness, and fitness?

Relationship Goals: What can I do today to improve my relationships?

Personal/ Professional Goals: What can I do today to reach my school, professional, business, or financial goals?

Celebrate Wins: What are you most proud of today?

Improvements: What changes are necessary now?

Date: _____

> **My Success Planner**
> **Take Action Every Day to Win**

Mindset Goals: What positive thoughts will I have today?
_____
_____
_____

Emotional Goals: What positive actions will I take today to feel joy and happiness?
_____
_____
_____

Health/ Fitness/ Wellness Goals: What can I do today to improve my health, wellness, and fitness?
_____
_____
_____

Relationship Goals: What can I do today to improve my relationships?
_____
_____
_____

Personal/ Professional Goals: What can I do today to reach my school, professional, business, or financial goals?
_____
_____
_____

Celebrate Wins: What are you most proud of today?
_____

Improvements: What changes are necessary now?
_____

Date: _____

**My Success Planner
Take Action Every Day to Win**

Mindset Goals: What positive thoughts will I have today?

Emotional Goals: What positive actions will I take today to feel joy and happiness?

Health/ Fitness/ Wellness Goals: What can I do today to improve my health, wellness, and fitness?

Relationship Goals: What can I do today to improve my relationships?

Personal/ Professional Goals: What can I do today to reach my school, professional, business, or financial goals?

Celebrate Wins: What are you most proud of today?

Improvements: What changes are necessary now?

Date: _____

> **My Success Planner**
> **Take Action Every Day to Win**

Mindset Goals: What positive thoughts will I have today?

Emotional Goals: What positive actions will I take today to feel joy and happiness?

Health/ Fitness/ Wellness Goals: What can I do today to improve my health, wellness, and fitness?

Relationship Goals: What can I do today to improve my relationships?

Personal/ Professional Goals: What can I do today to reach my school, professional, business, or financial goals?

Celebrate Wins: What are you most proud of today?

Improvements: What changes are necessary now?

Date: _____

**My Success Planner
Take Action Every Day to Win**

Mindset Goals: What positive thoughts will I have today?

Emotional Goals: What positive actions will I take today to feel joy and happiness?

Health/ Fitness/ Wellness Goals: What can I do today to improve my health, wellness, and fitness?

Relationship Goals: What can I do today to improve my relationships?

Personal/ Professional Goals: What can I do today to reach my school, professional, business, or financial goals?

Celebrate Wins: What are you most proud of today?

Improvements: What changes are necessary now?

Date: _____

**My Success Planner
Take Action Every Day to Win**

Mindset Goals: What positive thoughts will I have today?

Emotional Goals: What positive actions will I take today to feel joy and happiness?

Health/ Fitness/ Wellness Goals: What can I do today to improve my health, wellness, and fitness?

Relationship Goals: What can I do today to improve my relationships?

Personal/ Professional Goals: What can I do today to reach my school, professional, business, or financial goals?

Celebrate Wins: What are you most proud of today?

Improvements: What changes are necessary now?

Date: _____

My Success Planner
Take Action Every Day to Win

Mindset Goals: What positive thoughts will I have today?

Emotional Goals: What positive actions will I take today to feel joy and happiness?

Health/ Fitness/ Wellness Goals: What can I do today to improve my health, wellness, and fitness?

Relationship Goals: What can I do today to improve my relationships?

Personal/ Professional Goals: What can I do today to reach my school, professional, business, or financial goals?

Celebrate Wins: What are you most proud of today?

Improvements: What changes are necessary now?

Date: _____

**My Success Planner
Take Action Every Day to Win**

Mindset Goals: What positive thoughts will I have today?

Emotional Goals: What positive actions will I take today to feel joy and happiness?

Health/ Fitness/ Wellness Goals: What can I do today to improve my health, wellness, and fitness?

Relationship Goals: What can I do today to improve my relationships?

Personal/ Professional Goals: What can I do today to reach my school, professional, business, or financial goals?

Celebrate Wins: What are you most proud of today?

Improvements: What changes are necessary now?

Date: _____

My Success Planner
Take Action Every Day to Win

Mindset Goals: What positive thoughts will I have today?

Emotional Goals: What positive actions will I take today to feel joy and happiness?

Health/ Fitness/ Wellness Goals: What can I do today to improve my health, wellness, and fitness?

Relationship Goals: What can I do today to improve my relationships?

Personal/ Professional Goals: What can I do today to reach my school, professional, business, or financial goals?

Celebrate Wins: What are you most proud of today?

Improvements: What changes are necessary now?

Date: _____

> **My Success Planner**
> **Take Action Every Day to Win**

Mindset Goals: What positive thoughts will I have today?

Emotional Goals: What positive actions will I take today to feel joy and happiness?

Health/ Fitness/ Wellness Goals: What can I do today to improve my health, wellness, and fitness?

Relationship Goals: What can I do today to improve my relationships?

Personal/ Professional Goals: What can I do today to reach my school, professional, business, or financial goals?

Celebrate Wins: What are you most proud of today?

Improvements: What changes are necessary now?

Date: _____

**My Success Planner
Take Action Every Day to Win**

Mindset Goals: What positive thoughts will I have today?

Emotional Goals: What positive actions will I take today to feel joy and happiness?

Health/ Fitness/ Wellness Goals: What can I do today to improve my health, wellness, and fitness?

Relationship Goals: What can I do today to improve my relationships?

Personal/ Professional Goals: What can I do today to reach my school, professional, business, or financial goals?

Celebrate Wins: What are you most proud of today?

Improvements: What changes are necessary now?

Date: _____

My Success Planner
Take Action Every Day to Win

Mindset Goals: What positive thoughts will I have today?
_____
_____
_____

Emotional Goals: What positive actions will I take today to feel joy and happiness?
_____
_____
_____

Health/ Fitness/ Wellness Goals: What can I do today to improve my health, wellness, and fitness?
_____
_____
_____

Relationship Goals: What can I do today to improve my relationships?
_____
_____
_____

Personal/ Professional Goals: What can I do today to reach my school, professional, business, or financial goals?
_____
_____
_____

Celebrate Wins: What are you most proud of today?
_____

Improvements: What changes are necessary now?
_____

Date: _____

**My Success Planner
Take Action Every Day to Win**

Mindset Goals: What positive thoughts will I have today?

Emotional Goals: What positive actions will I take today to feel joy and happiness?

Health/ Fitness/ Wellness Goals: What can I do today to improve my health, wellness, and fitness?

Relationship Goals: What can I do today to improve my relationships?

Personal/ Professional Goals: What can I do today to reach my school, professional, business, or financial goals?

Celebrate Wins: What are you most proud of today?

Improvements: What changes are necessary now?

Date: _____

> **My Success Planner**
> **Take Action Every Day to Win**

Mindset Goals: What positive thoughts will I have today?

Emotional Goals: What positive actions will I take today to feel joy and happiness?

Health/ Fitness/ Wellness Goals: What can I do today to improve my health, wellness, and fitness?

Relationship Goals: What can I do today to improve my relationships?

Personal/ Professional Goals: What can I do today to reach my school, professional, business, or financial goals?

Celebrate Wins: What are you most proud of today?

Improvements: What changes are necessary now?

Date: _____

My Success Planner
Take Action Every Day to Win

Mindset Goals: What positive thoughts will I have today?

Emotional Goals: What positive actions will I take today to feel joy and happiness?

Health/ Fitness/ Wellness Goals: What can I do today to improve my health, wellness, and fitness?

Relationship Goals: What can I do today to improve my relationships?

Personal/ Professional Goals: What can I do today to reach my school, professional, business, or financial goals?

Celebrate Wins: What are you most proud of today?

Improvements: What changes are necessary now?

Date: _____

| My Success Planner
  Take Action Every Day to Win |

Mindset Goals: What positive thoughts will I have today?

Emotional Goals: What positive actions will I take today to feel joy and happiness?

Health/ Fitness/ Wellness Goals: What can I do today to improve my health, wellness, and fitness?

Relationship Goals: What can I do today to improve my relationships?

Personal/ Professional Goals: What can I do today to reach my school, professional, business, or financial goals?

Celebrate Wins: What are you most proud of today?

Improvements: What changes are necessary now?

Date: _____

**My Success Planner
Take Action Every Day to Win**

Mindset Goals: What positive thoughts will I have today?

Emotional Goals: What positive actions will I take today to feel joy and happiness?

Health/ Fitness/ Wellness Goals: What can I do today to improve my health, wellness, and fitness?

Relationship Goals: What can I do today to improve my relationships?

Personal/ Professional Goals: What can I do today to reach my school, professional, business, or financial goals?

Celebrate Wins: What are you most proud of today?

Improvements: What changes are necessary now?

Date: _____

**My Success Planner
Take Action Every Day to Win**

Mindset Goals: What positive thoughts will I have today?

Emotional Goals: What positive actions will I take today to feel joy and happiness?

Health/ Fitness/ Wellness Goals: What can I do today to improve my health, wellness, and fitness?

Relationship Goals: What can I do today to improve my relationships?

Personal/ Professional Goals: What can I do today to reach my school, professional, business, or financial goals?

Celebrate Wins: What are you most proud of today?

Improvements: What changes are necessary now?

Date: _____

**My Success Planner
Take Action Every Day to Win**

Mindset Goals: What positive thoughts will I have today?

Emotional Goals: What positive actions will I take today to feel joy and happiness?

Health/ Fitness/ Wellness Goals: What can I do today to improve my health, wellness, and fitness?

Relationship Goals: What can I do today to improve my relationships?

Personal/ Professional Goals: What can I do today to reach my school, professional, business, or financial goals?

Celebrate Wins: What are you most proud of today?

Improvements: What changes are necessary now?

Date: _____

My Success Planner
Take Action Every Day to Win

Mindset Goals: What positive thoughts will I have today?

Emotional Goals: What positive actions will I take today to feel joy and happiness?

Health/ Fitness/ Wellness Goals: What can I do today to improve my health, wellness, and fitness?

Relationship Goals: What can I do today to improve my relationships?

Personal/ Professional Goals: What can I do today to reach my school, professional, business, or financial goals?

Celebrate Wins: What are you most proud of today?

Improvements: What changes are necessary now?

Date: _____

> **My Success Planner**
> **Take Action Every Day to Win**

Mindset Goals: What positive thoughts will I have today?

Emotional Goals: What positive actions will I take today to feel joy and happiness?

Health/ Fitness/ Wellness Goals: What can I do today to improve my health, wellness, and fitness?

Relationship Goals: What can I do today to improve my relationships?

Personal/ Professional Goals: What can I do today to reach my school, professional, business, or financial goals?

Celebrate Wins: What are you most proud of today?

Improvements: What changes are necessary now?

Date: _____

> **My Success Planner**
> **Take Action Every Day to Win**

Mindset Goals: What positive thoughts will I have today?

Emotional Goals: What positive actions will I take today to feel joy and happiness?

Health/ Fitness/ Wellness Goals: What can I do today to improve my health, wellness, and fitness?

Relationship Goals: What can I do today to improve my relationships?

Personal/ Professional Goals: What can I do today to reach my school, professional, business, or financial goals?

Celebrate Wins: What are you most proud of today?

Improvements: What changes are necessary now?

Date: _____

My Success Planner
Take Action Every Day to Win

Mindset Goals: What positive thoughts will I have today?

Emotional Goals: What positive actions will I take today to feel joy and happiness?

Health/ Fitness/ Wellness Goals: What can I do today to improve my health, wellness, and fitness?

Relationship Goals: What can I do today to improve my relationships?

Personal/ Professional Goals: What can I do today to reach my school, professional, business, or financial goals?

Celebrate Wins: What are you most proud of today?

Improvements: What changes are necessary now?

Date: _____

My Success Planner
Take Action Every Day to Win

Mindset Goals: What positive thoughts will I have today?
_____
_____
_____

Emotional Goals: What positive actions will I take today to feel joy and happiness?
_____
_____
_____

Health/ Fitness/ Wellness Goals: What can I do today to improve my health, wellness, and fitness?
_____
_____
_____

Relationship Goals: What can I do today to improve my relationships?
_____
_____
_____

Personal/ Professional Goals: What can I do today to reach my school, professional, business, or financial goals?
_____
_____
_____

Celebrate Wins: What are you most proud of today?
_____

Improvements: What changes are necessary now?
_____

Date: _____

My Success Planner
Take Action Every Day to Win

Mindset Goals: What positive thoughts will I have today?

Emotional Goals: What positive actions will I take today to feel joy and happiness?

Health/ Fitness/ Wellness Goals: What can I do today to improve my health, wellness, and fitness?

Relationship Goals: What can I do today to improve my relationships?

Personal/ Professional Goals: What can I do today to reach my school, professional, business, or financial goals?

Celebrate Wins: What are you most proud of today?

Improvements: What changes are necessary now?

My Success Planner
Take Action Every Day to Win

Date: _____

Mindset Goals: What positive thoughts will I have today?

Emotional Goals: What positive actions will I take today to feel joy and happiness?

Health/ Fitness/ Wellness Goals: What can I do today to improve my health, wellness, and fitness?

Relationship Goals: What can I do today to improve my relationships?

Personal/ Professional Goals: What can I do today to reach my school, professional, business, or financial goals?

Celebrate Wins: What are you most proud of today?

Improvements: What changes are necessary now?

Date: _____

**My Success Planner
Take Action Every Day to Win**

Mindset Goals: What positive thoughts will I have today?

Emotional Goals: What positive actions will I take today to feel joy and happiness?

Health/ Fitness/ Wellness Goals: What can I do today to improve my health, wellness, and fitness?

Relationship Goals: What can I do today to improve my relationships?

Personal/ Professional Goals: What can I do today to reach my school, professional, business, or financial goals?

Celebrate Wins: What are you most proud of today?

Improvements: What changes are necessary now?

Date: _____

> **My Success Planner**
> **Take Action Every Day to Win**

Mindset Goals: What positive thoughts will I have today?

Emotional Goals: What positive actions will I take today to feel joy and happiness?

Health/ Fitness/ Wellness Goals: What can I do today to improve my health, wellness, and fitness?

Relationship Goals: What can I do today to improve my relationships?

Personal/ Professional Goals: What can I do today to reach my school, professional, business, or financial goals?

Celebrate Wins: What are you most proud of today?

Improvements: What changes are necessary now?

Date: _____

**My Success Planner
Take Action Every Day to Win**

Mindset Goals: What positive thoughts will I have today?

Emotional Goals: What positive actions will I take today to feel joy and happiness?

Health/ Fitness/ Wellness Goals: What can I do today to improve my health, wellness, and fitness?

Relationship Goals: What can I do today to improve my relationships?

Personal/ Professional Goals: What can I do today to reach my school, professional, business, or financial goals?

Celebrate Wins: What are you most proud of today?

Improvements: What changes are necessary now?

Date: _____

**My Success Planner
Take Action Every Day to Win**

Mindset Goals: What positive thoughts will I have today?

Emotional Goals: What positive actions will I take today to feel joy and happiness?

Health/ Fitness/ Wellness Goals: What can I do today to improve my health, wellness, and fitness?

Relationship Goals: What can I do today to improve my relationships?

Personal/ Professional Goals: What can I do today to reach my school, professional, business, or financial goals?

Celebrate Wins: What are you most proud of today?

Improvements: What changes are necessary now?

Date: _____

**My Success Planner
Take Action Every Day to Win**

Mindset Goals: What positive thoughts will I have today?

Emotional Goals: What positive actions will I take today to feel joy and happiness?

Health/ Fitness/ Wellness Goals: What can I do today to improve my health, wellness, and fitness?

Relationship Goals: What can I do today to improve my relationships?

Personal/ Professional Goals: What can I do today to reach my school, professional, business, or financial goals?

Celebrate Wins: What are you most proud of today?

Improvements: What changes are necessary now?

Date: _____

> **My Success Planner**
> **Take Action Every Day to Win**

Mindset Goals: What positive thoughts will I have today?

Emotional Goals: What positive actions will I take today to feel joy and happiness?

Health/ Fitness/ Wellness Goals: What can I do today to improve my health, wellness, and fitness?

Relationship Goals: What can I do today to improve my relationships?

Personal/ Professional Goals: What can I do today to reach my school, professional, business, or financial goals?

Celebrate Wins: What are you most proud of today?

Improvements: What changes are necessary now?

Date: _____

**My Success Planner
Take Action Every Day to Win**

Mindset Goals: What positive thoughts will I have today?

Emotional Goals: What positive actions will I take today to feel joy and happiness?

Health/ Fitness/ Wellness Goals: What can I do today to improve my health, wellness, and fitness?

Relationship Goals: What can I do today to improve my relationships?

Personal/ Professional Goals: What can I do today to reach my school, professional, business, or financial goals?

Celebrate Wins: What are you most proud of today?

Improvements: What changes are necessary now?

Date: _____

My Success Planner
Take Action Every Day to Win

Mindset Goals: What positive thoughts will I have today?

Emotional Goals: What positive actions will I take today to feel joy and happiness?

Health/ Fitness/ Wellness Goals: What can I do today to improve my health, wellness, and fitness?

Relationship Goals: What can I do today to improve my relationships?

Personal/ Professional Goals: What can I do today to reach my school, professional, business, or financial goals?

Celebrate Wins: What are you most proud of today?

Improvements: What changes are necessary now?

Date: _____

> **My Success Planner**
> **Take Action Every Day to Win**

Mindset Goals: What positive thoughts will I have today?

Emotional Goals: What positive actions will I take today to feel joy and happiness?

Health/ Fitness/ Wellness Goals: What can I do today to improve my health, wellness, and fitness?

Relationship Goals: What can I do today to improve my relationships?

Personal/ Professional Goals: What can I do today to reach my school, professional, business, or financial goals?

Celebrate Wins: What are you most proud of today?

Improvements: What changes are necessary now?

Date: _____

**My Success Planner
Take Action Every Day to Win**

Mindset Goals: What positive thoughts will I have today?

Emotional Goals: What positive actions will I take today to feel joy and happiness?

Health/ Fitness/ Wellness Goals: What can I do today to improve my health, wellness, and fitness?

Relationship Goals: What can I do today to improve my relationships?

Personal/ Professional Goals: What can I do today to reach my school, professional, business, or financial goals?

Celebrate Wins: What are you most proud of today?

Improvements: What changes are necessary now?

Date: _____

My Success Planner
Take Action Every Day to Win

Mindset Goals: What positive thoughts will I have today?

Emotional Goals: What positive actions will I take today to feel joy and happiness?

Health/ Fitness/ Wellness Goals: What can I do today to improve my health, wellness, and fitness?

Relationship Goals: What can I do today to improve my relationships?

Personal/ Professional Goals: What can I do today to reach my school, professional, business, or financial goals?

Celebrate Wins: What are you most proud of today?

Improvements: What changes are necessary now?

Date: _____

**My Success Planner
Take Action Every Day to Win**

Mindset Goals: What positive thoughts will I have today?

Emotional Goals: What positive actions will I take today to feel joy and happiness?

Health/ Fitness/ Wellness Goals: What can I do today to improve my health, wellness, and fitness?

Relationship Goals: What can I do today to improve my relationships?

Personal/ Professional Goals: What can I do today to reach my school, professional, business, or financial goals?

Celebrate Wins: What are you most proud of today?

Improvements: What changes are necessary now?

Date: _____

**My Success Planner
Take Action Every Day to Win**

Mindset Goals: What positive thoughts will I have today?

Emotional Goals: What positive actions will I take today to feel joy and happiness?

Health/ Fitness/ Wellness Goals: What can I do today to improve my health, wellness, and fitness?

Relationship Goals: What can I do today to improve my relationships?

Personal/ Professional Goals: What can I do today to reach my school, professional, business, or financial goals?

Celebrate Wins: What are you most proud of today?

Improvements: What changes are necessary now?

Date: _____

My Success Planner
Take Action Every Day to Win

Mindset Goals: What positive thoughts will I have today?

Emotional Goals: What positive actions will I take today to feel joy and happiness?

Health/ Fitness/ Wellness Goals: What can I do today to improve my health, wellness, and fitness?

Relationship Goals: What can I do today to improve my relationships?

Personal/ Professional Goals: What can I do today to reach my school, professional, business, or financial goals?

Celebrate Wins: What are you most proud of today?

Improvements: What changes are necessary now?

Date: _____

**My Success Planner
Take Action Every Day to Win**

Mindset Goals: What positive thoughts will I have today?

Emotional Goals: What positive actions will I take today to feel joy and happiness?

Health/ Fitness/ Wellness Goals: What can I do today to improve my health, wellness, and fitness?

Relationship Goals: What can I do today to improve my relationships?

Personal/ Professional Goals: What can I do today to reach my school, professional, business, or financial goals?

Celebrate Wins: What are you most proud of today?

Improvements: What changes are necessary now?

Date: _____

My Success Planner
Take Action Every Day to Win

Mindset Goals: What positive thoughts will I have today?

Emotional Goals: What positive actions will I take today to feel joy and happiness?

Health/ Fitness/ Wellness Goals: What can I do today to improve my health, wellness, and fitness?

Relationship Goals: What can I do today to improve my relationships?

Personal/ Professional Goals: What can I do today to reach my school, professional, business, or financial goals?

Celebrate Wins: What are you most proud of today?

Improvements: What changes are necessary now?

Date: _____

> **My Success Planner**
> **Take Action Every Day to Win**

Mindset Goals: What positive thoughts will I have today?

Emotional Goals: What positive actions will I take today to feel joy and happiness?

Health/ Fitness/ Wellness Goals: What can I do today to improve my health, wellness, and fitness?

Relationship Goals: What can I do today to improve my relationships?

Personal/ Professional Goals: What can I do today to reach my school, professional, business, or financial goals?

Celebrate Wins: What are you most proud of today?

Improvements: What changes are necessary now?

Date: _____

**My Success Planner
Take Action Every Day to Win**

Mindset Goals: What positive thoughts will I have today?

Emotional Goals: What positive actions will I take today to feel joy and happiness?

Health/ Fitness/ Wellness Goals: What can I do today to improve my health, wellness, and fitness?

Relationship Goals: What can I do today to improve my relationships?

Personal/ Professional Goals: What can I do today to reach my school, professional, business, or financial goals?

Celebrate Wins: What are you most proud of today?

Improvements: What changes are necessary now?

Date: _____

**My Success Planner
Take Action Every Day to Win**

Mindset Goals: What positive thoughts will I have today?

Emotional Goals: What positive actions will I take today to feel joy and happiness?

Health/ Fitness/ Wellness Goals: What can I do today to improve my health, wellness, and fitness?

Relationship Goals: What can I do today to improve my relationships?

Personal/ Professional Goals: What can I do today to reach my school, professional, business, or financial goals?

Celebrate Wins: What are you most proud of today?

Improvements: What changes are necessary now?

Date: _____

My Success Planner
Take Action Every Day to Win

Mindset Goals: What positive thoughts will I have today?

Emotional Goals: What positive actions will I take today to feel joy and happiness?

Health/ Fitness/ Wellness Goals: What can I do today to improve my health, wellness, and fitness?

Relationship Goals: What can I do today to improve my relationships?

Personal/ Professional Goals: What can I do today to reach my school, professional, business, or financial goals?

Celebrate Wins: What are you most proud of today?

Improvements: What changes are necessary now?

Date: _____

My Success Planner
Take Action Every Day to Win

Mindset Goals: What positive thoughts will I have today?

Emotional Goals: What positive actions will I take today to feel joy and happiness?

Health/ Fitness/ Wellness Goals: What can I do today to improve my health, wellness, and fitness?

Relationship Goals: What can I do today to improve my relationships?

Personal/ Professional Goals: What can I do today to reach my school, professional, business, or financial goals?

Celebrate Wins: What are you most proud of today?

Improvements: What changes are necessary now?

Date: _____

My Success Planner
Take Action Every Day to Win

Mindset Goals: What positive thoughts will I have today?

Emotional Goals: What positive actions will I take today to feel joy and happiness?

Health/ Fitness/ Wellness Goals: What can I do today to improve my health, wellness, and fitness?

Relationship Goals: What can I do today to improve my relationships?

Personal/ Professional Goals: What can I do today to reach my school, professional, business, or financial goals?

Celebrate Wins: What are you most proud of today?

Improvements: What changes are necessary now?

Date: _____

**My Success Planner
Take Action Every Day to Win**

Mindset Goals: What positive thoughts will I have today?

Emotional Goals: What positive actions will I take today to feel joy and happiness?

Health/ Fitness/ Wellness Goals: What can I do today to improve my health, wellness, and fitness?

Relationship Goals: What can I do today to improve my relationships?

Personal/ Professional Goals: What can I do today to reach my school, professional, business, or financial goals?

Celebrate Wins: What are you most proud of today?

Improvements: What changes are necessary now?

Date: _____

**My Success Planner
Take Action Every Day to Win**

Mindset Goals: What positive thoughts will I have today?
___
___
___

Emotional Goals: What positive actions will I take today to feel joy and happiness?
___
___
___

Health/ Fitness/ Wellness Goals: What can I do today to improve my health, wellness, and fitness?
___
___
___

Relationship Goals: What can I do today to improve my relationships?
___
___
___

Personal/ Professional Goals: What can I do today to reach my school, professional, business, or financial goals?
___
___
___

Celebrate Wins: What are you most proud of today?
___

Improvements: What changes are necessary now?
___

Date: _____

My Success Planner
Take Action Every Day to Win

Mindset Goals: What positive thoughts will I have today?

Emotional Goals: What positive actions will I take today to feel joy and happiness?

Health/ Fitness/ Wellness Goals: What can I do today to improve my health, wellness, and fitness?

Relationship Goals: What can I do today to improve my relationships?

Personal/ Professional Goals: What can I do today to reach my school, professional, business, or financial goals?

Celebrate Wins: What are you most proud of today?

Improvements: What changes are necessary now?

Date: _____

> **My Success Planner**
> **Take Action Every Day to Win**

Mindset Goals: What positive thoughts will I have today?

Emotional Goals: What positive actions will I take today to feel joy and happiness?

Health/ Fitness/ Wellness Goals: What can I do today to improve my health, wellness, and fitness?

Relationship Goals: What can I do today to improve my relationships?

Personal/ Professional Goals: What can I do today to reach my school, professional, business, or financial goals?

Celebrate Wins: What are you most proud of today?

Improvements: What changes are necessary now?

Date: _____

| My Success Planner |
| Take Action Every Day to Win |

Mindset Goals: What positive thoughts will I have today?

_____

_____

_____

Emotional Goals: What positive actions will I take today to feel joy and happiness?

_____

_____

_____

Health/ Fitness/ Wellness Goals: What can I do today to improve my health, wellness, and fitness?

_____

_____

_____

Relationship Goals: What can I do today to improve my relationships?

_____

_____

_____

Personal/ Professional Goals: What can I do today to reach my school, professional, business, or financial goals?

_____

_____

_____

Celebrate Wins: What are you most proud of today?

_____

Improvements: What changes are necessary now?

_____

Date: _____

My Success Planner
Take Action Every Day to Win

Mindset Goals: What positive thoughts will I have today?

Emotional Goals: What positive actions will I take today to feel joy and happiness?

Health/ Fitness/ Wellness Goals: What can I do today to improve my health, wellness, and fitness?

Relationship Goals: What can I do today to improve my relationships?

Personal/ Professional Goals: What can I do today to reach my school, professional, business, or financial goals?

Celebrate Wins: What are you most proud of today?

Improvements: What changes are necessary now?

Date: _____

My Success Planner
Take Action Every Day to Win

Mindset Goals: What positive thoughts will I have today?

Emotional Goals: What positive actions will I take today to feel joy and happiness?

Health/ Fitness/ Wellness Goals: What can I do today to improve my health, wellness, and fitness?

Relationship Goals: What can I do today to improve my relationships?

Personal/ Professional Goals: What can I do today to reach my school, professional, business, or financial goals?

Celebrate Wins: What are you most proud of today?

Improvements: What changes are necessary now?

Date: _____

> **My Success Planner**
> **Take Action Every Day to Win**

Mindset Goals: What positive thoughts will I have today?

Emotional Goals: What positive actions will I take today to feel joy and happiness?

Health/ Fitness/ Wellness Goals: What can I do today to improve my health, wellness, and fitness?

Relationship Goals: What can I do today to improve my relationships?

Personal/ Professional Goals: What can I do today to reach my school, professional, business, or financial goals?

Celebrate Wins: What are you most proud of today?

Improvements: What changes are necessary now?

Date: _____

**My Success Planner
Take Action Every Day to Win**

Mindset Goals: What positive thoughts will I have today?

Emotional Goals: What positive actions will I take today to feel joy and happiness?

Health/ Fitness/ Wellness Goals: What can I do today to improve my health, wellness, and fitness?

Relationship Goals: What can I do today to improve my relationships?

Personal/ Professional Goals: What can I do today to reach my school, professional, business, or financial goals?

Celebrate Wins: What are you most proud of today?

Improvements: What changes are necessary now?

Date: _____

My Success Planner
Take Action Every Day to Win

Mindset Goals: What positive thoughts will I have today?

Emotional Goals: What positive actions will I take today to feel joy and happiness?

Health/ Fitness/ Wellness Goals: What can I do today to improve my health, wellness, and fitness?

Relationship Goals: What can I do today to improve my relationships?

Personal/ Professional Goals: What can I do today to reach my school, professional, business, or financial goals?

Celebrate Wins: What are you most proud of today?

Improvements: What changes are necessary now?

Date: _____

**My Success Planner
Take Action Every Day to Win**

Mindset Goals: What positive thoughts will I have today?

Emotional Goals: What positive actions will I take today to feel joy and happiness?

Health/ Fitness/ Wellness Goals: What can I do today to improve my health, wellness, and fitness?

Relationship Goals: What can I do today to improve my relationships?

Personal/ Professional Goals: What can I do today to reach my school, professional, business, or financial goals?

Celebrate Wins: What are you most proud of today?

Improvements: What changes are necessary now?

Date: _____

My Success Planner
Take Action Every Day to Win

Mindset Goals: What positive thoughts will I have today?

Emotional Goals: What positive actions will I take today to feel joy and happiness?

Health/ Fitness/ Wellness Goals: What can I do today to improve my health, wellness, and fitness?

Relationship Goals: What can I do today to improve my relationships?

Personal/ Professional Goals: What can I do today to reach my school, professional, business, or financial goals?

Celebrate Wins: What are you most proud of today?

Improvements: What changes are necessary now?

Date: _____

**My Success Planner
Take Action Every Day to Win**

Mindset Goals: What positive thoughts will I have today?

Emotional Goals: What positive actions will I take today to feel joy and happiness?

Health/ Fitness/ Wellness Goals: What can I do today to improve my health, wellness, and fitness?

Relationship Goals: What can I do today to improve my relationships?

Personal/ Professional Goals: What can I do today to reach my school, professional, business, or financial goals?

Celebrate Wins: What are you most proud of today?

Improvements: What changes are necessary now?

Date: _____

My Success Planner
Take Action Every Day to Win

Mindset Goals: What positive thoughts will I have today?

Emotional Goals: What positive actions will I take today to feel joy and happiness?

Health/ Fitness/ Wellness Goals: What can I do today to improve my health, wellness, and fitness?

Relationship Goals: What can I do today to improve my relationships?

Personal/ Professional Goals: What can I do today to reach my school, professional, business, or financial goals?

Celebrate Wins: What are you most proud of today?

Improvements: What changes are necessary now?

Date: _____

> **My Success Planner**
> **Take Action Every Day to Win**

Mindset Goals: What positive thoughts will I have today?

Emotional Goals: What positive actions will I take today to feel joy and happiness?

Health/ Fitness/ Wellness Goals: What can I do today to improve my health, wellness, and fitness?

Relationship Goals: What can I do today to improve my relationships?

Personal/ Professional Goals: What can I do today to reach my school, professional, business, or financial goals?

Celebrate Wins: What are you most proud of today?

Improvements: What changes are necessary now?

Date: _____

**My Success Planner
Take Action Every Day to Win**

Mindset Goals: What positive thoughts will I have today?

Emotional Goals: What positive actions will I take today to feel joy and happiness?

Health/ Fitness/ Wellness Goals: What can I do today to improve my health, wellness, and fitness?

Relationship Goals: What can I do today to improve my relationships?

Personal/ Professional Goals: What can I do today to reach my school, professional, business, or financial goals?

Celebrate Wins: What are you most proud of today?

Improvements: What changes are necessary now?

Date: _____

**My Success Planner
Take Action Every Day to Win**

Mindset Goals: What positive thoughts will I have today?

Emotional Goals: What positive actions will I take today to feel joy and happiness?

Health/ Fitness/ Wellness Goals: What can I do today to improve my health, wellness, and fitness?

Relationship Goals: What can I do today to improve my relationships?

Personal/ Professional Goals: What can I do today to reach my school, professional, business, or financial goals?

Celebrate Wins: What are you most proud of today?

Improvements: What changes are necessary now?

Date: _____

> **My Success Planner**
> **Take Action Every Day to Win**

Mindset Goals: What positive thoughts will I have today?

Emotional Goals: What positive actions will I take today to feel joy and happiness?

Health/ Fitness/ Wellness Goals: What can I do today to improve my health, wellness, and fitness?

Relationship Goals: What can I do today to improve my relationships?

Personal/ Professional Goals: What can I do today to reach my school, professional, business, or financial goals?

Celebrate Wins: What are you most proud of today?

Improvements: What changes are necessary now?

Date: _____

**My Success Planner
Take Action Every Day to Win**

Mindset Goals: What positive thoughts will I have today?

Emotional Goals: What positive actions will I take today to feel joy and happiness?

Health/ Fitness/ Wellness Goals: What can I do today to improve my health, wellness, and fitness?

Relationship Goals: What can I do today to improve my relationships?

Personal/ Professional Goals: What can I do today to reach my school, professional, business, or financial goals?

Celebrate Wins: What are you most proud of today?

Improvements: What changes are necessary now?

Date: _____

**My Success Planner
Take Action Every Day to Win**

Mindset Goals: What positive thoughts will I have today?

Emotional Goals: What positive actions will I take today to feel joy and happiness?

Health/ Fitness/ Wellness Goals: What can I do today to improve my health, wellness, and fitness?

Relationship Goals: What can I do today to improve my relationships?

Personal/ Professional Goals: What can I do today to reach my school, professional, business, or financial goals?

Celebrate Wins: What are you most proud of today?

Improvements: What changes are necessary now?

Date: _____

> **My Success Planner**
> **Take Action Every Day to Win**

Mindset Goals: What positive thoughts will I have today?
_____
_____
_____

Emotional Goals: What positive actions will I take today to feel joy and happiness?
_____
_____
_____

Health/ Fitness/ Wellness Goals: What can I do today to improve my health, wellness, and fitness?
_____
_____
_____

Relationship Goals: What can I do today to improve my relationships?
_____
_____
_____

Personal/ Professional Goals: What can I do today to reach my school, professional, business, or financial goals?
_____
_____
_____

Celebrate Wins: What are you most proud of today?
_____

Improvements: What changes are necessary now?
_____

Date: _____

> **My Success Planner**
> **Take Action Every Day to Win**

Mindset Goals: What positive thoughts will I have today?

Emotional Goals: What positive actions will I take today to feel joy and happiness?

Health/ Fitness/ Wellness Goals: What can I do today to improve my health, wellness, and fitness?

Relationship Goals: What can I do today to improve my relationships?

Personal/ Professional Goals: What can I do today to reach my school, professional, business, or financial goals?

Celebrate Wins: What are you most proud of today?

Improvements: What changes are necessary now?

Date: _____

My Success Planner
Take Action Every Day to Win

Mindset Goals: What positive thoughts will I have today?

Emotional Goals: What positive actions will I take today to feel joy and happiness?

Health/ Fitness/ Wellness Goals: What can I do today to improve my health, wellness, and fitness?

Relationship Goals: What can I do today to improve my relationships?

Personal/ Professional Goals: What can I do today to reach my school, professional, business, or financial goals?

Celebrate Wins: What are you most proud of today?

Improvements: What changes are necessary now?

Date: _____

> **My Success Planner**
> **Take Action Every Day to Win**

Mindset Goals: What positive thoughts will I have today?

Emotional Goals: What positive actions will I take today to feel joy and happiness?

Health/ Fitness/ Wellness Goals: What can I do today to improve my health, wellness, and fitness?

Relationship Goals: What can I do today to improve my relationships?

Personal/ Professional Goals: What can I do today to reach my school, professional, business, or financial goals?

Celebrate Wins: What are you most proud of today?

Improvements: What changes are necessary now?

Date: _____

**My Success Planner
Take Action Every Day to Win**

Mindset Goals: What positive thoughts will I have today?

Emotional Goals: What positive actions will I take today to feel joy and happiness?

Health/ Fitness/ Wellness Goals: What can I do today to improve my health, wellness, and fitness?

Relationship Goals: What can I do today to improve my relationships?

Personal/ Professional Goals: What can I do today to reach my school, professional, business, or financial goals?

Celebrate Wins: What are you most proud of today?

Improvements: What changes are necessary now?

Section 5

Reflections and Wins

Taking time to reflect on your progress and wins is critical to achieve success. Reflection is a time to think about the victories and changes that are necessary to win. Success is built on wins, mistakes, challenges, change, and growth.

In this section you can take time to learn from past experiences and mistakes. Mistakes teach us how to do things differently to get better results. During your reflections, you can also think about new strategies that can drive you forward. Take note of new ideas and partnerships that can move you forward towards your success.

Reflection Questions

- What did you learn today? What wins are you having?
- What changes are necessary to move you forward?
- Who can help you achieve your next goal?
- How can you provide better services?
- What are some challenges or difficulties you are currently facing?
- What fears or doubts are you experiencing?
- How can you change your relationships to get better results?
- Who can provide resources or information to help you?
- How can you conclude your current project?
- How will you feel when you achieve your new goals?
- What is keeping you up at night?
- How will you celebrate when you achieve your goals?
- How do you hope to inspire others?

WINS/VICTORIES

WINS/VICTORIES

Made in the USA
Columbia, SC
29 May 2023